V E R M I L I O N

by

Alan Britt

The Bitter Oleander Press
Fayetteville, New York
13066-9776
USA

2006

The Bitter Oleander Press
4983 Tall Oaks Drive
Fayetteville, New York 13066-9776
USA

www.bitteroleander.com
info@bitteroleander.com

Copyright © 2006 by Alan Britt

First Edition

All rights reserved.

No part of this book may be used or reproduced in any manner whatsoever without written permission except in the case of brief quotations embodied in critical articles and reviews.

Manufactured in the United States of America

Printed by McNaughton & Gunn, Inc.
Saline, MI

Graphic Design & Layout:
Roderick Martinez Visual Communications
Liverpool, New York

Cover painting by Ultra Violet: *The wedding of masculine and feminine angels or the passion of aesthetic* (Mix medium — 3 D collage — silver leaf — acrylic paint — gold leaf...In permanent collection of "Le Petit Palais," Paris)...
www.ultravioletweb.com

ISBN# 0-9664358-8-5

Library of Congress Control Number: 2005903314

VERMILION

ACKNOWLEDGMENTS

Grateful acknowledgment is made to editors of the publications in which the following poems first appeared:

Ann Arbor Review (Internet): "Spanish Villa," "Listening to Vivaldi's Concerto for Two Mandolins While Driving to Work," and "Wooden Gate";
The Aurorean: "Relaxing in the Backyard with Shasta"; *
Birmingham Poetry Review: "The Snow Leopard";
The Bitter Oleander: "Yellow Tile," "Icy Wind," "A Life," "White Leopard," "Winter Garden," "April Night," and "Bird Voices";
Cold Mountain Review: "Lilies";
Connecticut River Review: "White Jasmine";
Latino Stuff Review: "Blackbirds";
Long Island Quarterly: "Venus";
Montserrat Review: "Magician," and "Growing Old";
New Letters: "Neighbor";
Parnassus Literary Journal: "Politics";
Poetry Depth Quarterly: "Twilight";
Puerto del Sol: "Wooden Gate";
Voodoo Souls Quarterly: "Leopards"

---

* "Relaxing in the Backyard with Shasta," first appeared in *The Great American Poetry Show 1*, Larry Ziman, Editor, The Muse Media, West Hollywood, CA: 2004.

For my mother, Roberta Crawford,
who's done more than anyone to educate the public
about the dangers of iron overload.
www.ironoverload.org

TABLE OF CONTENTS

PART ONE

The Snow Leopard	11
Himalaya	12
Puritan Wife	13
No One Knows Its Taste	14
Elemental Gods	15
Neighbor	16
Jerusalem	17
Amusing	18
Yellow Tile	20
White Jasmine	21
Joni Mitchell	22
Gin & Tonic	23
A Poem About the Momentary	24

PART TWO

Icy Wind	27
Lilies	28
A Life	29
Queen of Spades	30
Eat This Poem	32
White Leopard	33
Illusion & Life	34
Jack Casey	35
The Wall	36
Panic Existence	37
Death's Eyes	38
Vermilion	39
Watching a Movie	40
The Old Days	41

PART THREE

April Night	45
Winter Garden	46
Early Garden	48
Myth of the Baker's Daughter	50
Blackbirds	52
Listening to Vivaldi's Concerto for Two Mandolins While Driving to Work	53
A Mask Is Removed to Reveal the Human	54
Venus	56
Magician	57
Growing Old	58
The Robin Returns	60
Twilight	62

PART FOUR

Leopards	65
Relaxing in the Backyard with Shasta	66
Listening to Dogs	68
Wooden Gate	70
June Evening	71
Dream Atoms	72
Song of the Earth	74
Bird Voices	75
Neighbors	76
Roses	77
Tiny Spider	78
Politics	79

O N E

One night the soul of wine was singing in its bottles:
"Mankind, to you I send, dear disinherited,
From prison walls of glass with their vermilion stopples,
Songs of enlightenment and songs of brotherhood.

I know how much is needed on the scorching hill,
How much pain and how much sweat and fierce sunshine,
To propogate my life and furnish me my soul;
And I shall never be ungrateful or malign."

— Charles Baudelaire

THE SNOW LEOPARD

Monks take their pilgrimage
through the ghostly dunes
of a snow leopard's fur.

Their capes flow like muscular lava
down steep crags.

The ibex is primarily Buddhist,
balancing all points of existence
on a jagged edge.

The snow leopard digests the wisest part
of the blue sheep
in his long, elegant tail.

HIMALAYA

Ravens, vultures, eagles form an extended family
& greet one another with familial tension.

Bearded vultures shatter the tepid mountain
& devour the marrow
of a Buddhist mantra.

Blue footprints cross the forehead
of the Himalayas.

The snow leopard isn't water,
as much as we would like him to be,
but a nerve ending
orbiting, endlessly, orbiting.

PURITAN WIFE

In the macaque's mane
you'll find weather
two centuries old.

And parting the brief fog
of the macaque's mask
reveals Walt Whitman's footstep.

Now, lean closer. Do you feel the cold needle
of the abused Puritan wife,
stitching the blue flames
of her inner life?

NO ONE KNOWS ITS TASTE

— Miguel Hernández

Twisting the kitchen clock's brass key
I release a white pelican
from Einstein's fog.

Freed, it pursues
existence on this side.

Nadie sabe su sabor.

How true.
Our sense of taste
is momentary,
volatile.

The white pelican flies
across our living room
then disappears around a dusty corner
into our sad dining room.

A dining room
lit by four red candles,
two of them imprisoned behind Cubist mosaics
of peacock-blue stained-glass.

Nadie sabe su sabor.

How true.
No one knows.
How true!

ELEMENTAL GODS

If every living cell in our universe
is a soul feeding,
then the human brain is still light years
away from tasting the sap
of a blue spruce.

As I see it,
nothing less than 100%
brain cell activation
is required to even marginally
qualify us as elemental gods.

NEIGHBOR

My neighbor raking leaves,
bent, curled, crab apple leaves,
won't talk about death.

He's too young yet.

A minor stroke can't possibly
be his link to the universe.

But I say,
he hates those leaves.

What else is left?

JERUSALEM

I lived in a cramped space,
not because I liked it
but because I loved the people.

Living conditions
were atrocious
to anyone familiar
with indigo dragonflies
sifting Indiana clover.

I coughed in the face
of discretion.

I loved the Hebrew
forehead,
Egyptian hips
of solid earth.

We hid thousands
of scrolls
in the lungs
of our hives.

We wanted to remember
sisters, cousins, lovers,
mysterious confidants.

In a fraction
of a second,
I lived in a cramped space,
not because I liked it
but because I loved the people.

AMUSING

1.

You could easily crush my heart
beneath little fists of anger.

You could squeeze dirty light
from my brain.
Fashion my light waves
into your own clothes.
You are a designer
absorbing our cramped universe
into your impetuous moods.

You could easily crush my heart,
there's no doubt.

2.

A man narrates long, passive afternoons.
What does this man do for a living
that he gets paid to investigate our universe?
He relaxes against a jade pillow,
one supple hour of serenity.

3.

February is your bride.

She drags her veil of fog.

4.

You could easily crush all my light
beneath your tiny fists of anger.

YELLOW TILE

Surrounded by walls
of yellow tile.

A hive.

Paper echoes.

Am I inside
or out?

WHITE JASMINE

I have been severely decapitated.

Pursuant to suspicion,
I leapt headlong
into a crocodile
who had Chianti for lunch.

Salad, with a Greek oil
asleep in its leaves.

It took me forever to escape.

A violin,
with rusted dragonfly wings
for strings,
crouches below white jasmine.

JONI MITCHELL

Joni Mitchell sings,
textured as magnolia buds
in February.

Tight, feathery,
olive.

Her twisted black branches,
iconoclastic right down
to their chilly roots.

GIN & TONIC

America's blue-eyed boy
        epitomi(zed)
                bY
sTRuc
      t
            u
                r
                    e,
sToPpEd by for gin & tonic.

A POEM ABOUT THE MOMENTARY

How could you not love
this night?

Rain floods the lizard throats
of the gutters
around our white house.

Damp silence!

Outside, coolness
regulates the human brain.

Inside, a five-bladed ceiling fan
stirs the warm air
with just a hint of salmon
overflowing the oven.

T W O

Trying to shovel smoke with a pitchfork in the wind.

— John Lennon

ICY WIND

An icy wind
sweeps snow
like dust
from a swing-set's metal bones.

The kitchen window leaks.

Immediately I crank the window.

It opens
like a fresh gill.

LILIES

Everything we do is digression.

I could digress,
but...

Instead as I ease my head
inside the kitchen wall-clock's glass case,
one chime
instantly
vibrates my fleshy atoms.

Below a white ceiling fan
light drips
down frosted globes
that resemble five lilies.

The lilies chime
exactly three times.

A LIFE

A life
gives itself
to you.

Do you feel
its infinite blade?

QUEEN OF SPADES

1.

A blonde Italian strolls
through this room.

Champagne curls,
neoclassic nudity!

Lust crosses
these black & white tiles.

Renaissance lovers
are tame
compared to your
avocado waist!

2.

But South American smoke
& cigars like harmonicas
shadow the faces of the dead.

I told you I loved you.
Remember?

3.

Did you ever really know?

Surely you
suspected?

But did we
actually exchange lives?

4.

I wish I could feel you now.

Atoms of consciousness count,
don't they?

EAT THIS POEM

Your thighs of rope.

Every twitch
draws me closer
to hemp consciousness.

I might as well
eat this poem.

WHITE LEOPARD

Black tail.

White leopard,
my brain stretched across
your formica counter.

God, these moments
of illusion
are simply irresistible.

So, what do you think
this life cycle
meant to your dead grandmother?

Do you feel
her skin
on your bones now?

ILLUSION & LIFE

You can't please
everyone.

Cat's got my tongue
full of lies,
or flies,
you choose.

No one ever
warned me that bones
couldn't tell time,
could only predict the weather.

So I grew feet
that dangled at the ends
of brass clock bones.

Eventually amphibian claws
scratched their initials
into my blood.

JACK CASEY

I remember Jack Casey.

Jack Casey once created a nude
whose thick sensual legs
destroyed reason.

Violent acrylic
scraped onto canvas.

Yeah, I remember Jack.

His young lust devoured
the wild fibers
of raw canvas.

THE WALL

You talk
about the wall.

Shit!
Talk to Silvia.

She'll give you the wall
plus yellowblack
wings of freedom.

Every man,
every woman,
every swallowtail butterfly,
except those predisposed
to culturally
cultivated mentors.

Talk to me,
fine,
but don't hoard
all the shame;
some of us are starving.

I'll climb your mountain
of flesh,
of yellow cacti,
with an umbrella of innocence
shielding us from the only
true joy we've ever known.

PANIC EXISTENCE

Everything you say
presupposes
that life is hardly a whisper
in the pale green surf.

White guitar on your hip.

Hobnail boots with mirrors.

So, reveal
your desperate shoulders,
smooth shadows
of ice melting,
as good as any lover
devoured
by panic existence.

DEATH'S EYES

— for Damniso Lopez

The elder poet
writes about death.

Death is a clown,
a clown who misbehaves
according to preconception.

Or so we think.

Death can be windy,
blustery,
creaking the ribs of this small Toyota,
& unpredictable
like a vole reflected
off an owl's eye.

Death has too many hiding places.

My friend, the elder poet,
cradles death's wrist
looking for a pulse.

Unfortunately, once death's quartz-blue eyes,
like those on an antique, ceramic German doll
roll open, they never close.

VERMILION

The sun reclines
upon your eyelids,
makes you see vermilion.

The sun is heavy today
even though the wind
is furious about something.

Several Debussy oboes
don't understand
this feral wind.

They float alone,
two feet
above the orchestra
& could easily disappear
without ever realizing
what ripped them
from their ancestral sensibilities.

This morning
the sun wears a silk gown,
with hand-painted women
collecting green bamboo.

These women, arms loaded,
dark almond eyes,
weigh more some days
than others.

WATCHING A MOVIE

The actress's eyes are brilliant & dark
like those found in Flemish paintings
from the Age of Darkness.

Barely a frayed thread
of golden melancholy.

Her voice, of course,
is raw silk.

And, naturally, there is talk of valor.
Each gentlemen's cuff measured perfectly.
Faces flicker in spit-shine leather.

But the actress's eyes remain untouchable,
like two scarabs hiding
behind the Sahara's dirty blonde hair.

THE OLD DAYS

Remember when old books
meant old money?

Lots of old books.

When old books lined the walls
of musty game rooms,
billiards under gas light?

Angels fainting in the waist
of brandy?

Buzzards of smoke circling
fat Cuban cigars?

THREE

*the bird
stares
with small black eyes
like seeds
or buttons*

*at something
outside the scene
we cannot see*

— Isabel Fraire

APRIL NIGHT

Cicadas, invisible, almost atonal,
mine the stone darkness
with their humid choir.

Syncopated, they pause.

Theirs is the blood flow
of alien sensibility.

The tips of their drills
cut stars.

They create an entire village
beneath cool, thick clover.

Remember, they are not so much
romantic crooners
for our pleasure
as they are philosophers
for dreaming ants.

WINTER GARDEN

Squash bones litter the winter garden.

Imagination begins as a mussel,
grows inside its glistening black shell,
sunk waist-deep in the Gulf.
Black wings slowly open
but the mussel does not fly.
As a matter of fact,
the mussel does not move at all
until imagination cracks the seams
of its tiny black universe.
Tiny black pupil that feeds the brain.
Tiny black universe.
Tiny black seed.

Squash bodies lie in freezing rain,
corpses floating on black waves
of glistening oil.

The mussel wants to fly.
The mussel wants to run.

Eventually, it sinks below the surf;
its green hair extends
from Florida to Cuba,
Pensacola to Habana.

Then thin black shoulders emerge from the white hair
of salt water. They

look me straight in the eyes
& rattle dry tamarind seeds
inside those squash corpses
I dreamt about
when I was a boy.
But now I am a man.
It is my job to examine
teeth marks carved on the Renaissance shells
abandoned by the souls of these squash.

EARLY GARDEN

Just past ten in the morning,
overcast,
white dew
sparkles broccoli leaves.

Infant broccoli plants,
fatherless,
no aunts, uncles,
except for onions, garlic,
yellow tomatoes,
ruby lettuce
that surround them.

Over the next five months
this garden & I
will enjoy a life cycle.

I'll watch over the garden daily,
strolling the shadow
of my grandfather,
lifting the opulent rhubarb leaf,
waiting for the white bud
to signal the arrival
of a twisted green pepper
& watching fireflies linger
near the basil.

My grandfather, Melvin,
in his faded-brown t-shirt

placed boards as pathways
throughout his Tampa garden.
Every tomato, cabbage, carrot
received his Democratic attention.
Each grapefruit tree, tangerine, lime,
plum & lemon thrived at his touch.

I inherited my late grandfather's love
for gardens.
Now I celebrate various roots, mysterious vines,
yellow cucumber flowers.

Even as I emerge a little late this morning,
the white dew on cabbage leaves
resembles sweat on Granddad's forehead,
or sunlight through the straw hat
crumbling around his eyes.

MYTH OF THE BAKER'S DAUGHTER

They say the owl
used to be a baker's daughter
with wild hyacinth hair.

As a matter of fact,
people were barely able to detect any color
at all in her flowing hair.

Her legs were smoke,
although many believed she consisted entirely
of water.

She spent much time pleasing & nurturing,
as you would expect from a baker's daughter.

This went on for several thousand years.
Her life-span was a drop of quicksilver.

Then came the day when her services
no longer pleased;
the world had completely forgotten her.

Eventually, the world created a new job for her, though.
It now needed her to clean rodents
from death's teeth.

But she never complained.

Over the course of time,
perhaps several more millennia,
the world lost
complete control
of her muscular arms
& without warning
her arms evolved into bronze feathers.

Tonight, on the cool branch of a midnight pine,
sits an owl
who used to be a baker's daughter.

BLACKBIRDS

Blackbirds prowl the yard,
tug a worm or two from white clover,
wander between broccoli & lettuce,
then lower themselves into puddles.

A cowbird, with elegant rusted head,
pursues a female.
She rebuffs him twice
before they finally fly away together.

Two robins enter the garden
competing for warms, though heavily outnumbered
by the exquisite blackbirds
who displace the robins at will.

The May wind blows cold across my arm
as I watch three blackbirds
easing their hypodermics
through the overcast sky.

LISTENING TO VIVALDI'S CONCERTO FOR TWO MANDOLINS WHILE DRIVING TO WORK

Two mandolins
stir my coffee.

Two geese fly
across the road
directly above me.
Green necks outstretched
as though threading
their souls
through the expansive eye
of the infinite.

A MASK IS REMOVED TO REVEAL THE HUMAN

May breeze.

Three empty white chairs below the scarlet mouths
of pink magnolias.

Late shadows stretch their dark muscles
across tall grass.

The breeze delivers two clouds,
the waft of azalea,
& arias of sparrows, mockingbirds, finches.

These mysteries are absorbed through my skin,
along with a solitary violin
& thick dandelions.

As the afternoon settles,
it is a busy time
for everything around me.

Two walkers stride past our wooden fence,
our split-rail fence
faded silverbrown.

I could die in this breeze,
but I could thrive also
as maple seeds plop like rain
& yellow light bulbs splatter brick porches.

At the uppermost tip of a tall thin spruce
a tiny bird
like a particle of ash
attaches itself to a branch in my universe.

A ruby-headed finch drinks
from a faded-melon-colored dog bowl.

I am fortunate to be fed, nourished,
by these invisible currents of May.

Gradually I release toxins
into the breeze,
odorless, colorless toxins
that rise from the dampness
in my bones.

Out of nowhere a goshawk's
fanned tail
swoops low through my universe.

Its grey stripes
vaporize the twilight.

For a moment, at least,
for a minor crumb of eternity,
it seems I have forgotten all worldly complaints
& returned to my senses.

VENUS

Venus eats the sky,
the elephant sky.

The walls of a small universe
collapse.

Stucco walls the color of mango.

Why?

Venus strolls.

Her hips of silk
push aside
thick clouds.

Venus eats the elephant sky.

Venus parts her lips
of spotted leopards
against my chest,
my chest
of dead oboes.

Every atom from her soft lips
is a crushed river
full of acid & silk.

MAGICIAN

On one fingertip
a magician balances an elephant.

Our entire universe
is sleight-of-hand.

Of course,
if you're paying close attention
you already know this.

A dog barks in the distance,
six houses away.

He sounds like a basset hound
with drooping, half-moons
for eyes.

GROWING OLD

Pastel sky.

Delicate clouds, yes,
like pipe smoke
wafting from the pages of a thousand-year-old
German fairy tale.

When I was younger
I could dive into the soft blue.
But now, I simply
lack the energy.

I can't borrow the required anger from Baudelaire,
or employ the impossible precision of Mallarmé.

I no longer know how to get there.

Maybe I don't want to get there.
Maybe I don't want to disappear
into the void.
Maybe I'm too lazy,
or maybe I'm curiously
fueled
by a robin igniting the end
of a faded tomato stake.

I can talk to the robin
& he listens.
He tolerates my intrusion
into his hunt for worms.

He returns,
over & over,
Over & over.

I say the same thing
each time
in a bird language
I've learned
from catbirds, finches, cardinals,
& glorious mockingbirds.

The robin tolerates my existence;
perhaps he's even curious,
by the way he twists his head
at odd angles,
connecting my solitude
to his routine.

I no longer have a routine.
I've lived long enough
to discover something beyond
my pitiful self,
my pathetic cravings.
I've outlived the routine
I inherited a lifetime ago.

Much to my surprise.

THE ROBIN RETURNS

The robin returns.

He's been back
six times,
seven times.

Goes to the same spot,
a puddle
between lettuce & peppers
in my garden.

I know what he's up to
now.

He carries away
a beak full of wet grass;
heads straight
to our silver maple.

I know what he's doing.

He's securing the walls
to his adobe nest.

He'll return at least
two more times
before I fall asleep
in my midnight-blue lounge chair
embroidered with mauve flowers.

See.

He returns.

Only this time
he pulls some dried grass
from beneath the sawed branches
of our dead dogwood.

Our unfortunate dogwood
that now resembles
a bleached cow skull
discarded
along the vermilion sands
of a Georgia O'Keefe painting.

TWILIGHT

Twilight.

Leaves rustle
like dense silk
discarded
by a nude lover.

Green lover,
blue-grey eyes
the breeze
against my legs.

FOUR

...however
        why not acknowledge
that myth for example
              is a language
    that now
           because it is alien
                seems suggestive
              mysterious
            rich
              truer than others
only because its grammar is unknown to us?

— Isabel Fraire

LEOPARDS

Leopards hunt best
under
a black moon.

Leopards patrol
a difficult niche.

Although their spots
far outnumber
hyena stars.

Utter darkness
stirs their liquid souls.

RELAXING IN THE BACKYARD WITH SHASTA

Two rosy finches
chase one another
through dark branches.

Lime fireflies
vaporize above the clover.

Shasta,
our black Bouvier,
settles
like smoke
upon the clay roots
of a maple.

Her ears twitch
as catbirds
negotiate
the young darkness

Fireflies
prowl the hedges.

A streetlight
tightens her corset,
breathes deep
while balancing on one dark leg.

Shasta sighs,
shifts her weight.

An imperceptible breeze
vibrates
the longest
grey tuft
of her silky beard.

LISTENING TO DOGS

Leaves hiss.

Dogs bark
from three different directions.

Another,
possibly small & white,
joins them
from inside a house.

Now a hound,
with a complaint
that sounds like he awoke
just in time
to catch something
eating his dream,
digesting it bite by bite
while he slept.

An elm leg creaks,
a sparrow trills,
& from a new direction
yet another invisible dog
releases his bark
into the loose folds of the evening.

By now there must
be eight dogs
or more

forming a chain of voices
inside the cool arteries
of this neighborhood,

& every so often,
when you lean forward,
you'd swear
a new bark, yelp or howl
barely vibrates these Debussy clouds
of twilight.

WOODEN GATE

June opens
her lusty mouth.

A white cayenne
pepper blossom
trembles
between the green shoulders
of narrow leaves.

A wooden gate
rattles the latch,
its cool handcuffs
of insomnia.

JUNE EVENING

A moth,
the size
of a fingernail,
color
of a faded board,
navigates
the tall clover.

A house finch
pursues,
missing once
then recalculates
perfectly,
before racing
like a tiny trail of smoke
across the yard.

DREAM ATOMS

Twilight again.

It's always twilight
when dream atoms
dance wildly.

My life
is in
these atoms.

One
resembles grief
filled with seaweed.
Another
bruises the hip
of the first one,
then oozes like an overripe grape.
A third
weightless,
electric,
drifts through a rottweiler's teeth
one block away.

A fourth!
A Fifth!
Hundreds
like bees
split

the abdomen
of this cool summer evening!

Tonight
I navigate
by smell only.

Soon
I'll be
the only
living panther
in suburban Maryland.

SONG OF THE EARTH

She collapses
like ash
onto the wooden floor.

Gustav Mahler breathes
the air
of a dead orchid,
or metal
that survives
just under the tongue.

She collapses
like ash
caught in the muscular throat
of insomnia.

Gustav inhales
air
through a tiny hour-glass.

BIRD VOICES

      A yellow & black swallowtail butterfly dances a complete alphabet around me. Cardinals are quite shy. A beautiful orange female hops across the shingled roof of my neighbor's white tool shed, before disappearing into oven humidity below a nearby oak.
      The sweet odor of decaying grass in the compost pile resembles the woodwind moan of a mourning dove. The mourning stops, replaced by occasional squawks from a grackle, perhaps a crow, but more likely a mockingbird. A long, metallic sound gives the mockingbird away. Bird voices are now as thick as abundant leaves. The only difference is you can't see the birds, though their nuances embroider immanentist branches across the sky.

NEIGHBORS

     A man in red shirt bends to
prune a bush against his brick house.
His red burns a hole through humidity.
     A wild sprinkler darkens his wall
below a white window with black shutters.
     The man examines his bush. Afraid
it will die from drought, or afraid it will
burst into flames? This is America. I believe
he is more afraid of what the neighbors
might think.

ROSES

      A blonde woman drags a green garden hose across the backyard. Bending over, she leaves very little to the imagination.

      In the next yard, roses hang like fists of blood.

TINY SPIDER

      This tiny vermilion spider crawls
upon me for the third time. With my fingertip
uneasily yet gently I've set him down each time.
This time, however, I find him wandering aimlessly,
hopelessly lost at the center of my poem.

POLITICS

Elephants
wage political war,
planning well in advance,
presuming their latest maneuver
will be long forgotten
at the ballot box.

The Donkeys,
who at least
have a sense of humor,
respond
accordingly.

About the Author

Alan Britt teaches English at Towson University. His recent books are *Infinite Days* (The Bitter Oleander Press: 2003), *Amnesia Tango* (Cedar Hill Publications: 1998), and *Bodies of Lightning* (Cypress Books: 1995). Essays and poetry have recently appeared in *Arson* and *Clay Palm Review*. Interviews along with his poetry have also recently been featured in *Steaua* (Romania), *Latino Stuff Review*, and *Poet's Market*. Other poems have appeared in *Christian Science Monitor, Confrontation, English Journal, Epoch, Flint Hills Review, Fox Cry Review, Kansas Quarterly, Magyar Naplo* (Hungary), *Midwest Quarterly, New Letters, Pacific Review, Puerto del Sol, Queen's Quarterly* (Canada), *Revista Solar* (Mexico), *Sou'wester, Square Lake*, plus the anthologies, *Fathers: Poems About Fathers* (St. Martin's Press: 1998) and *La Adelfa Amarga: Seis Poetas Norteamericanos de Hoy* (Ediciones El Santo Oficio, Peru, 2003).

~ ~ ~

Other books by Alan Britt:

The Afternoon of the Light
I Suppose the Darkness Is Ours
Ashes in the Flesh
I Ask for Silence, Also